PRAISE FOR *THE WAITING PERIOD*

"Brilliant...Positively Inspirational!"
—*San Francisco Chronicle*

———————

"*The Waiting Period* is ultimately as life-affirming
a show as you could hope to see."
—*Chad Jones Theater Dogs*

THE WAITING PERIOD

a memoir of depression

Brian Copeland

THE WAITING PERIOD

a memoir of depression

Brian Copeland

Book design by Dorothy Carico Smith

This book is respectfully dedicated to the memories of
Colton Fink (1995-2011)
Matthew Christopher Potthast (1996-2015)
and Robin Williams (1951-2014)

"Never put a period where God has placed a comma."

—*Gracie Allen*

INTRODUCTION

"**W**hy can't you just snap out of it?"
"Don't you know how lucky you are?"
"Get over it."
"Stop being such a drama queen. It's not the end of the world."

I don't think that there's a person alive who suffers from depression who has not heard some iteration of the above from well meaning (and sometimes not so well meaning) friends, family and acquaintances. The idea that extreme sadness can be the result of a medical issue is a difficult concept for a lot of people to wrap their heads around. Despite the fact that an estimated 16 million Americans (6.9% of the population) and 350 million people worldwide have at least one depressive episode in any given year, there is a broad misunderstanding about what the disease is and the devastating effect that it has on the sufferer. This lack of understanding has perpetuated the stigma attached to depression. It is a stigma that is costing lives.

We have an epidemic of depression and suicide in America.

It is the third leading cause of death among 15 to 24 year-olds, taking high school and college kids who don't know how to deal with the despair that they're feeling. It overwhelms underdeveloped minds, racked with an excruciating pain that can't accurately be articulated to anyone. As a teen, I was one of them.

In high school, I was a gregarious, funny, outgoing and sociable kid. I was always acting in plays, running for student government, organizing dances and going to parties. Most people who knew me back then would be astonished to learn that during that four year period, I doubt there was a day that I wasn't suicidal. There wasn't a day that I stood at a crosswalk waiting for the light to change that I didn't think to myself, "If I just step off the curb a little early, it can be all over."

Though the depression subsided to some degree as I got older, it periodically rears its head, plunging me into agonizing bouts of despair that have at times literally brought me to my knees.

For the afflicted, depression is like the tide. It ebbs and flows. On the best days it is at bay. Under control. On the worst days, it grabs me by the throat, throws me on the bed and sits on top of me, bearing down with its full weight, refusing to let me up.

In 2008, a series of calamities threw me into the worst bout of depression I'd ever known. It was a relentless and agonizing anguish that I almost didn't survive. After I came out the other side, I decided to share the story of that bout with two goals in mind. The first was to get people who are on the brink to open up and tell somebody how they're feeling in order to get help and support before it's too late. The second was to try and help family and friends of depressives (as well as the public at large) to develop a greater understanding of what those who battle the disease go through. I wanted to give folks the opportunity to see what the world looks like through the eyes of someone who is suicidally depressed. It is only with this kind of comprehension that we can erase the shame of mental illness and thus, save lives.

With these goals in mind, I approached my stage director and collaborator David Ford. David was the guiding force behind my first solo play, Not a Genuine Black Man. I told him what I had in mind; a play about a suicidal bout of depression that entertained while also acting as a theatrical intervention of sorts. A piece that mixed laughter, tears, empathy and information. We developed The Waiting Period and it opened at The Marsh theater in San Francisco in 2012. It was well received by critics, but more importantly, it was well received by people who have difficulty explaining to others what's going on inside of them during the dark times.

If you are "one of us," I hope that your takeaway from the following story is this: TELL SOMEONE. If I can publicly spill my guts to strangers both on stage and in print, you can tell someone that you are having thoughts that are not in your best interests. If you struggle, I promise you that there is a light at the end of the tunnel. I don't know how long it will be before you see that light. I can't promise that you will see it in a day, a month or even a year. What I can promise is that if you bail, if you take your life, you'll never see it. Suicide is a permanent solution to a temporary problem.

Depression is a demon whispering in your ear. It's giving you false information in order to hurt you. Don't let it. And don't try to fight it alone. Rely on family and friends. If they don't understand (which is often the case) use the resources of professionals. There is no shame in asking for help.

If you are someone who happens to care about "one of us," keep your antennae up. We can be the best liars in the world when it comes to hiding our true feelings. "I'm fine," is an answer that is often untrue. As you read the following pages, see if you recognize the behavior in anyone you know. If you do, check in with them. Keep an eye on them. Most importantly, intervene if necessary. Trust me when I say that you'll be saving a life.

CHAPTER 1

I think that at some point we have all entered places that we really didn't want to be seen going into. Places that make you question the very core of who you are. Like the unemployment office. Or a strip club. WalMart. A Justin Bieber concert.

"I'm only here because it's my daughter's birthday. What do you mean, 'where is she?'"

For parents of young children, I think the pharmacy is the worst place. They don't want the world to know that their kid is the one with the head lice as they surreptitiously attempt to sneak the lice medicine out of the store. I've read that black people can't get head lice. Apparently the lice don't care to live in *those* neighborhoods.

We're always so concerned about people judging us. I once bought a $150 shirt because I needed condoms. I was in the gift shop of a swanky San Francisco hotel and the clerk was an older woman who reminded me of the nuns I endured in grammar school. When she asked what I needed, the last thing I could do with my Catholic guilt was come right out and ask for rubbers. Instead, I tried the ancient verbal camouflage trick.

"Yes, I'd like that shirt," I said, pointing to a rack of designer garments behind her, "some condoms and that snow globe of the Golden Gate Bridge because it looks so...realistic."

In spite of all of this, eventually there comes a time when you throw caution to wind and say, "Fuck what people think." But, not today.

These were the thoughts that swirled through my mind as I stood in front of the big steel door with black iron bars. I glanced from side to side, praying that nobody I knew was strolling in the vicinity or driving by. The last thing I wanted getting around was that I'd been seen going into *that* place.

I have been fortunate as a playwright, writer, actor, comic and radio/television host in gaining notoriety. While I've had some good fortune on the national stage, I am most prominent in the San Francisco Bay Area where I'm well known after twenty odd years of coming into the homes and cars of residents via the airwaves. It's great to be recognized a lot of the time. When you want to privately go about your business, not so much. When you've achieved even a minor celebrity, it's amazing how much you're watched, even when you aren't aware of it.

I remember once going for a walk in a local park. I was enjoying a beautiful spring day when behind me, I heard a woman's voice say, "Two eggs over medium, home fried potatoes no onions, dry rye toast and black coffee."

I turned around to see a slender middle aged woman I didn't recognize.

"I'm sorry?" I said.

"I'm a waitress at the diner downtown," she said. "You came

in for breakfast a couple of years ago and that's what you ordered."

Now, I don't remember ever visiting that particular diner, but this woman nailed my favorite breakfast so I took her at her word. More importantly, it underscored how scrutinized I was in the region, even when I wasn't aware of it in the moment. Thus, the last thing I needed in the liberal Bay Area was for somebody to recognize me entering door in front of me.

A copper doorbell with a black button was affixed directly to the right of the door. I pressed it to hear a much too loud ding-dong. A few seconds later, the door vibrated with a buzzer so loud that it rattled my teeth. As I heard the doorknob click, I quickly turned it and pried the heavy metal door open enough to enter. Once inside, I let the door go and it shut with a CLANG. So much for being discreet.

I paused for a second and took in my surroundings. The place was not what I had expected at all. It was so tiny. So cluttered. It was not what I had thought that a gun shop was going to look like. To my left were a few dozen photos of various men posing proudly with the carcases of deer that they'd just blasted into oblivion. I guess that's because deer are so threatening.

To my right was a big poster of Osama Bin Laden with the circles of a target drawn over his face. As if anybody coming in here would have been able to nail the guy it took 48 Navy Seals to get. On the adjacent wall was the obligatory Confederate flag, thumb tacked to the wall, giving it all of the respect that it deserves in my opinion.

I've never understood people who have an affinity for the Confederacy. They'll say to you, "Hey, that's a part of our heritage!"

I never knew that the words 'heritage' and 'treason' were interchangeable. Personally, I think that anybody who loves the Confederate flag should only be paid in Confederate money. Then, let's see how committed they really are to this premise.

The wall behind me was a makeshift collage of bikini clad models packing heat, trying very hard to look lethal and sexy at the same time. I don't know how you pull that off. I've been married twice. They were either lethal or sexy. Never both.

I walked through the store, past camouflage clothes and racks of recent copies of *'Gun's and Ammo'* and stopped in front of a large glass cabinet. Behind it was a guy who, to me anyway, looked like he drives a tractor to his gig at the feed store. He was a lanky young man in his twenties wearing a John Deere hat and a Pendleton shirt. The bizarre thing was that he was smoking. I thought that gunpowder was supposed to be flammable.

The lit cigarette danced between his lips as he talked to an older gentleman leaning with one arm resting on the side of the counter. I could tell that this gun store was the equivalent of the local barbershop for this man. He wore a plaid shirt that unbuttoned just enough to display a gold nugget necklace resting in a gray birds' nest of chest hair. Nothing like a man who knows how to accessorize.

I call that nugget jewelry, "lazy ass" jewelry because that's exactly what it is. I picture a guy in a gold mine with a pick in one hand and a gold nugget in another saying, "Look what I found! I can melt this down and make…nah, I'll just put it on a chain."

I walked up to the glass counter and the tractor guy took one look and me, smiled and said, "Duuuude!" in a cadence that reminded me of Spicoli in. Where the hell did that come from?

"Can I, like help you dude?"

"Well," I said, fumbling for the right words, "I'd like to look at your revolvers please."

Let me fess up and say that I know nothing about guns. Nothing. I DO know 'revolver' though. It's a Beatles' album.

"I'd like to see your revolvers please."

"Aw dude," he said, disappointment creeping into his voice. Where was this guy from that he looked like a walking Skoal ad but sounded like a refugee from a Frankie and Annette movie.

"You should have been here earlier," he said. "I just sold my last .38 this morning."

"Oh," I said. "Well, do you have anything smaller? Like a …37?"

The Nugget Man chimed in, "What exactly do you need the weapon for?"

I love how gun guys always refer to their firearms as "weapons". Like they're talking about spears or swords or something.

"There have been some robberies in my neighborhood and I want to protect my family and…exercise my second amendment right to keep and bear arms," I said. "Like they say on Fox News."

When in Rome.

"I can certainly understand that," the Nugget Man said, each syllable leaving his throat as a growl.

The Surfer/Tractor guy reached into the glass cabinet, pulled out a small black pistol and handed it to me. It was tiny. Almost like a toy. I was wondering where the caps came out. I was entranced. I had never held a gun in my hands before and it felt cool. It was like I was holding a little, black steel penis extender. Not everybody can afford a Corvette.

"That's a .32 Baretta TomCat," Surf Dude said.

The Nugget Man added, "That one's a four chamber."

I looked at the gun in my hand and nodded. I had no idea what they were talking about.

"Aluminum alloy frame. Stainless steel slide and barrel. Holds seven rounds to a lip," he continued.

"How much?" I said, not looking up from the weapon in my hand. Great, now I'm saying "weapon".

"Well,' the Surf Dude said, "that one's used so I can cut you like a deal. How about $439."

"I can handle that," I said. "What's the procedure?"

"First, we gotta put you through like a background check to make sure that you're not like a terrorist or something."

A terrorist? With that little gun? What did they think I might do? Hijack a model airplane? "Okay, background check," I repeated. "That it?"

"Then there's the safety test, thirty questions," he said. "You're allowed to miss seven and still pass."

There's a test? Really?? I know guys who admire the I.Q.s of Rhesus monkeys who own gun collections. I don't think we're talking about the SAT here.

"Okay," I said. "Safety test. That it?"

"Then there's the ten-day waiting period," he said.

"Ten days?"

"Dude, it's the law," he said.

"God Damned People's Republic of California," the Nugget Man spat.

Ten days. The same time that TV schlock-meisters tell you they can teach you how to speak a new language. Ten days. The same time frame as credit card grace periods and inaccurate long range weather forecasts. Ten lousy days.

"Dude," he said trying to save his sale. "I'll even throw in your first clip. Seven rounds."

Seven bullets. If I couldn't figure out things in the next ten days…I would only need one.

CHAPTER 2

The alarm on my cellphone was piercing. If it hadn't been, I'm not sure that it would have cut through the sludge that was my brain in sleep that morning. I picked up the phone and checked the time. Eleven in the morning. Now what? The first thing that they tell you is to go about your normal routine. "Don't sit and dwell," they say. "Go out and be around people." Truth be told, I don't like being "around people" even when I don't feel like this.

It was Tuesday. Grocery shopping day. I usually cooked dinner for my three children every night, but I just hadn't had it in me in recent weeks. There wasn't even any food in the house, so I'd been ordering a lot of Chinese takeout. You know, if they ever do find a cure for depression, Chinese takeout is fucked.

Have you ever noticed how fortune cookies aren't really "fortune" cookies anymore? They're more like "compliment" cookies. When I was a kid, they used to say things like, "The woman of your dreams is nearby." Now they say "You're wearing a nice shirt." Thanks. It cost a hundred and fifty bucks.

Spaghetti is my daughter's favorite. I figured that I could get it together enough to boil some noodles so, I headed to Safeway. It was a gray, overcast day. The darkness of the noon sky was the perfect metaphor for my mood. I parked and got out of the car. I didn't remember the drive to the store. It was like I'd gotten behind the wheel, flipped a switch for autopilot and then zoned out, returning to that hollow void inside of me that I now called "home".

I grabbed a cart from the parking lot and went inside. I was in a haze as I picked up spaghetti, a jar of pre-made marinara sauce and a one-pound package of ground turkey. As I placed the turkey in the basket, I flashed on how I'd recently read that shopping carts have more germs than public toilets. Disgusting. The reason cited was that people sit their Huggy wearing babies in the cart and the children leave behind traces of fecal matter.

I was lost in my head, debating whether I should eat the turkey I'd just put in that nasty ass basket or if I should find an actual porcelain bowl to lick, when I heard a voice behind me.

"Hi Brian."

I turned around to see Roger, the "superdad" at my kids' school. You know the one. His wife works and makes a lot of money so he's the stay at home parent. This means that he approaches every aspect of the job like he's an executive at a Fortune 500 company. Nothing is done "part way". Now, this would be fine if he didn't take it to the extreme. Roger volunteers for *everything*. Then, because of his competitive nature, he does a much better job than you would have done had you been given this task that you didn't really want in the first place.

I've often wondered if this "can do" persona of his was overcompensation. It is the twenty-first century, but there are still sexist ideas about the roles of men and women in society. That being the case, it must be hard for Roger being in this situation. His wife is the breadwinner and everybody knows it. I wonder if this pushes him to try and display his masculinity.

"Hi Roger," I said. I didn't stop moving. I wanted the exchange to be a "walk and talk". No time or mood for chit chat.

"How are you," he said, breaking into a grin that showed off his perfectly capped, brilliantly white teeth.

Why do people ask that question? Nobody cares how you are. They just want you to say, "fine" so they can move on. It ranks up there with, "Does this dress make me look fat?" I learned a long time ago never to ask old people how they are because they'll actually tell you.

"Well, my daughter just got divorced and her twelve year-old has been smoking crack. She afraid I'm gonna break my hip on the stairs."

I'm gonna break your hip myself if you don't MOVE ON.

"I'm fine Roger. How are you?"

As soon as the words left my mouth I regretted them. I was now trapped in the frozen food section.

"We're having the charity bake sale for Hurricane Katrina refugees tomorrow. How about bringing in some cupcakes?" He said.

Why me? He was standing two aisles from them.

"Sure. How many do you need?"

"Oh," he said, stroking his chin and looking off into space like he was contemplating some question of monumental importance. "I think three dozen ought to do it."

Three dozen. Charity through the promotion of childhood

obesity. Only in America.

"Okay," I said, seeing a window to escape. "I'll get them. Good seeing you."

"Thanks," he said. "I'm off to rescue a kitten stuck in a tree."

As he wheeled his cart away, I half expected to see him open his shirt to reveal a bright red cape.

I went to the baked good section and got the cupcakes, then headed to the dairy section. When I got to the milk cooler, I grasped the handle and froze. It was cold, hard steel in my hand. Just like the Beretta. Nine more days.

I felt the little energy I had in my body slip away as I left the basket of groceries in the middle of the aisle and walked out of the store.

—

An hour and a half later, I sat in my shrink's office. My shrink at that time was one of those people who is so incredibly nice that it seems fake. The funny thing is that he *really* is sincere and he really is *that* nice.

"Hi Brian," he said, saccharine dripping from the word. "How are you?"

Again with the "how are you"?

"Fine," I stammered. "I'm just fine."

"Now Brian, we talked about this. Depression is just anger turned inward. I need you to take care of yourself and you won't take care of somebody you're mad at. So I'm gonna ask you again. How are you?"

"I'm fine," I said. "Really. I don't even think I'm depressed anymore."

"Not depressed huh?" He said. Skeptical. "No thoughts of suicide?"

It's been said that the two people you never want to lie to are your doctor or your lawyer. It could end in a death sentence.

"No," I said as I looking him in the eye. "No thoughts of suicide."

The suicidally depressed are probably the best liars in the world. They can cover what they're really feeling. They can go through the motions and appear to the outside world as though they are fine. As though they are going about life as usual and making it through the day. No one can tell that they are plotting horrible things in the dark recesses of their minds. Not until it's too late.

It's the reason most suicides come as a shock to the loved ones of the person who was so deeply in pain.

"No thoughts of suicide," I repeated, shaking my head.

"Good," he said.

I think I saw him exhale. Relieved.

"Now,", he said, "What have you had to eat today?"

"Eat?"

"Yes, eat," he said. "You know, "chow down". It's a part of getting better you know."

Shit. I forgot to eat.

"Let's see…for breakfast I had eggs benedict with asparagus tips and hollandaise sauce. Lunch was a beef wellington in a puff pastry followed by crème broulet for dessert."

He arched an eyebrow.

"You had this where?" He asked. Again, skeptical.

"Denny's," I said. "I had a coupon."

His tone changed. He didn't like it when I was flip.

"Listen," he said. "This depression isn't gonna cure itself. I can't help you if *you* won't help you."

I wondered if it ever occurred to him that maybe, I didn't really want him to help me.

—

As I walked into the house, my cell phone lit up. I looked at the caller ID. My friend Chuck.

"Hey man," he said. "How are you?"

I lost it.

"Why does everybody keep asking me that?" I screamed. "I'm fine. I'm just fucking fine."

"Whoa man, chill."

"Sorry."

"I'm just checking on you man," he said. "Wanna make sure you're okay. You know, not rattling around in an empty house."

The demon grabbed the phone from me.

"I'm fine, I will be even *more* fine if people will just stop asking me how in the hell I am!"

Silence.

"I'm gonna call you later," he finally said. "Give you some time to smoke the bug out of your ass."

—

Dinner. Since I bailed on the spaghetti, it was Chinese take-out. My son Adam had a school function so it was just me, Carolyn and Casey. Carolyn was just Chatty Cathy, prattling on in that incessant way that 16 year old girls do. A million words a minute without so much as taking a breath.

"So Mindy said, if you want to write an article about the prom dress code, you also have to write one about prom fashions". I said, "I don't *want* to write about prom fashions, I only want to write about the prom dress code." She said, "Well I'm the editor, and I say that you can't write about the prom dress code unless you're gonna write about prom fashions too. Bitch."

Casey, my youngest, was twelve. In those days, he didn't say much. He just sat there...and smelled. You know how twelve-year-old boys have that odor? It's like hormones or something. They stink when they get out of the shower. When I was twelve, I couldn't stand to smell myself.

On more than one occasion, I've had the misfortune of being trapped in a car with four or five twelve-year-old boys. It's enough to gag a maggot.

"Daddy," Carolyn said, watching me quietly use my chopsticks to push my chow fun noodles back and forth across my plate, "Are you listening to me?"

I feigned a smile.

"Every word."

She looked into my eyes. My late mother's name was Carolyn too. I couldn't successfully lie to her either.

"Daddy, you look sad," She said. "How are you?"

I sighed.

"I'm just tired. That's all."

We finished dinner, cleared the table and I headed up to my room. My big, quiet, empty room. If I closed my eyes and I tried really hard, I could just catch a faint whiff of her scent. She hadn't been in that room in months and I could still smell her. I stood in front of her empty closet, looking at wire hangers that were strewn about the floor, all tangled together like some kind of Chinese puzzle that needed solving, the voices of the day repeating over and over in my head, *How are you? How are you?' How are you? How are you?*

Not so good. In fact, not good at all.

INTERLUDE: CHARLIE'S STORY

As told to the author

My name is Charlie and I'm fifteen. I always tease my dad that he really wanted a boy, because why would he call me Charlie when my name is Charlotte? That's okay. I love my dad. We used to play this game. You see, Mom always drank milk with every meal, so we'd compete to make her laugh because she'd pass the milk through her nose. The first one to see a trickle of milk come out of Mom's nose and yell, "cow" was the winner. I remember this one time, Dad came down to breakfast in just his shirt and tie and no pants. No pants! So, he sits down like everything is all normal and then, just as Mom's taking a sip, Dad says, "Is there a draft in here?" Mom lost it. She's all laughing and coughing and choking and milk is flying out of her nostrils. I yelled "cow!". Good times.

"Cow." Yeah, we called her that. Dad called her that too. Not to her face you know. Like, Mom said I was too young to wear makeup so I'd put it on at school. Sometimes I'd come home and forget and Dad would say, "You better go wash your

face before the Cow sees you." Stuff like that. It had nothing to
do with her weight. She was skinny as a rail. It was just a joke. I
wonder if that's why she left? It was so weird. I never saw them
fight or anything. Dad wouldn't yell if he was on fire. I came
home from school and her clothes were all gone and Dad that
she couldn't face me because it was too hard for her. She just
hoped that someday I'd realize that she wasn't really cut out to
be a wife and a mother and I'd understand. Then, Dad looked
at me like he thought I was gonna cry. I just asked if we could
get some pizza.

So, a couple months of the "new normal" went by and I was
doing my homework. History. *Ugh*. It"s like stuff that happened
before I was even born. I'm not gonna need this. I'm gonna be
an artist. It's not like I'm gonna go to a gallery and they're gonna
say, "We want to buy all your paintings, but first you have to
tell us who invented the cotton gin?" Obviously some guy who
couldn't paint.

So I'm tearing through this boring section on the Industri-
al Revolution and my finger sticks to the page. I lick it and it's
all coppery. It's really bleeding. Guess I got a paper cut. It hella
hurt. So I put a band aid on it and I go back to the Industri-
al Revolution, but the whole time my finger is like *throb throb
throb*.

A couple weeks later the Sadie Hawkins was coming up. You
know, the dance where the girls ask the boys? I decided I was
gonna ask Richard. You see, in algebra, he's all looking at me
but he's acting like he's not all looking at me but I know he is
because I'm looking at him too. Don't judge me. Anyway, I told
my friend Shelly who turned out *not* to be my friend because
then she went and asked Richard to the Sadie and Richard said

'yes'. That was totally jacked. I was really mad so I got my history book and started running my fingers all over the pages. Have you ever *tried* to give yourself a paper cut? It's just frustrating. So I had to find a blade.

First, I got one of those knives that Mom bought from QVC. I figured if it could cut a tin can in half and still slice a tomato, my skin wouldn't be a problem. So, I used the tip to make just a little cut on my forearm. The knife turned out to be really sharp. Too sharp. There was blood everywhere. At first, I thought I'd have to have my dad take me to the hospital, but I bandaged it myself. Not a Band Aid either. A real gauze bandage. I hid it under a long-sleeved shirt.

Shortly after that, we were having tryouts for the play. We were doing *Grease*. I wanted to try out for Rizzo because Richard was gonna try out for Kenickie. I was so right for that part, so I practiced being a bitch for like three weeks. But Shelly was bigger bitch because she's a *real* bitch. She got Rizzo and Richard got Kenickie and I had to watch Shelly the slut hang all over Richard. It was hard. I found razor blades in some old toiletries that mom left and they worked pretty good. Well, until I accidentally cut my finger while trying to cut my arm. I'm so not gonna be a surgeon.

Then one day, I was sitting in art class. It was one of those deals where you have to take a bunch of junk and make a work of art in an hour. I was having a crappy day because Dad was mad at me for forgetting to to the dishes. Then I got blood on my silk blouse, and I was late to school trying to get the blood out of my blouse. Then that A-hole Mr. Deeter gave me a detention for being late. Anyway, I'm in art class cutting through a piece of balsa wood with an Exacto knife and I notice how easy it cuts. When the bell rang, I dropped it in my backpack.

Then we had this heat wave. Over a hundred every day. I was wearing my white sweater one day and Dad says, "Why you wearing that? It's too hot."

I said, "I'm cold".

Then, I looked at my sleeve, and there was a red spot. And it was spreading. Dad said, "Show me your arm."

I got all defensive.

"What do you think? That I'm like a junkie or something?

"Show me your arm."

I pulled up my sleeve and…it's the first time I ever saw my dad cry.

CHAPTER 3

I was awakened from a restless sleep by the rain pounding against my bedroom window. It made me think of Grandma and how she always said that she could predict the rain by the arthritis in her knee. The thought made me smile. Then, I remembered. Grandma's gone now too. Grandma raised me after my mom died. The realization that she was gone made my stomach drop. It was like the first dip of a roller coaster or that feeling you get when you hear that you're going to be fired or your wife says she's leaving.

Asleep, you forget. And then you wake up and you remember and your intestines are suddenly in your feet. The funny thing is that people will actually say to you, "Why don't you just stop despairing? Perk up and stop despairing!"

That's like telling somebody with the flu, "Why don't you stop throwing up? If you'd just quit puking, you'd be fine!"

My body ached all over. Even my hair hurt. I decided that I would spend the day in bed. Maybe if I stayed there, nothing bad would happen. I longed for the Beretta.

I picked up my cellphone to check the time and it lit up. I never had have my ringer on *ever*. If I turn it on, I know that I'll forget to turn it off and I don't want to be *that guy*. You know the one, with the cellphone going off in church or at the doctor's office or in the theater. I don't want to be the person people look at and think, "What part of please silence your phone is unclear?"

Chuck's number appeared in the phone's caller ID bar.

"Hey man," he said. I could hear his brotherly concern even in those two words.

"Hey," I said.

"Well," he said, "You certainly sound more lifelike today."

"Fuck you."

I heard him chuckle.

"And back to normal too," he said. "I'm just checking on you man."

"I don't need you to check on me because I'm fine," I snapped.

"Your wife took off," he said, "You totaled your car, your grandmother died and you just had major surgery. Man you are in such denial."

"Well you'd certainly know. You're the king of denial," I said through clinched teeth.

"Oh Bullshit," he laughed.

"What about high school," I said. "What about Karen Phillips?"

His turn to clinch teeth.

"She was not a lesbian."

I laughed.

"You caught her in bed with another girl."

I heard him draw in a big breath.

"She was...experimenting."

"Oh," I said chuckling, "She was wearing a lab coat? *Denial.*

There was silence on the other end for a few seconds before he said, "Patricia Jackson."

There was a name I hadn't heard in years.

"What?" I asked. "She was just having a rough day."

"She slashed her wrists."

"I'd call that having a rough day."

His turn to laugh.

"And I'd call that denial," he said.

"Well what about you," I said. "Two six packs and a half a fifth of bourbon a day, but you were a social drinker."

A pause.

"Yeah," Chuck said. "That was denial. But I took care of my problem. When you gonna take care of yours?"

I became angry and defensive.

"I don't have a problem," I yelled into the phone, "Other than people continuing to try and tell me that I've got some kind of a goddamned problem."

"Relax," he said. "Let it go. Surrender to your Higher Power."

Oh Lord. Here we go.

Ever since Chuck stopped drinking, he's been much happier and certainly more in control of his life and I'm very proud of him. The problem is that we all have friends like this. During the first months of their recovery, you can't say a word without them finding a way to relate it to Alcoholics Anonymous.

YOU: Oh God it's raining. I hate the rain.

THEM: Accept the things you cannot control.

YOU: Just because I can't control it, doesn't mean that

I've got to like it.

THEM: It'll all be fine if you'll just surrender to your Higher Power.

Now is it me, or does AA stuff sound a lot like something out of Star Wars? Can't you just hear?

YODA: Do or do not. There is no try. To your higher power you must surrender.

Sometimes, I look at Chuck and think, "Man, what happened to you?" In high school this is the guy who used to hang out at Planned Parenthood to meet girls.

"Dude," I'd say, "That is *so* wrong."

"Hey," he'd reply. "These chicks are here for birth control. If you want money, you go to the bank right?"

Hard to argue with *that* logic.

I may be guilty of a lot of things, but denial isn't one of them. My grandmother was the ultimate realist. That woman pulled no punches and told you the truth whether you wanted to hear it or not.

I remember when was 16 and the high school yearbooks came out. There is an awful picture of me in the yearbook that year. Just terrible. When you're 16, that's the most important thing in the world. I came home and showed it to Grandma and I was very upset.

"Grandma, look at this picture of me. It's awful. It's horrible. It's terrible!" I whined.

She replied, "Well the camera can't take nothin' but what's in front of it. What you expect the camera to do?

Thank you for your kind support.

And, as for 'surrendering to my Higher Power', I'm Catholic. I'm confused enough. I'm a comic. If you want to do stand-up, you have to be a Catholic or a Jew. It's in the bylaws. I'm really a "Cafeteria Catholic". I get a tray, I get in line and say, "I'll take some of this doctrine, a little of that Vatican dictate. You can keep the homophobia. I'm glad that gay people can get married. Why should they get to be happy?"

"I'm sorry," I said. "You just caught me at a bad moment. That's all."

"I just want you to know that I'm here for you," Chuck said. "If you need anything, even just to bullshit, I'm here."

"I appreciate that. I really do. In fact, I'm gonna go out for a run. Right now."

"Good," he said. "That would be good for you."

"Alright. Let me get out of here before I lose my motivation," I said.

"Alright. Now you call me later, okay?"

"I will," I said, knowing full well that I wouldn't.

I would go running though. I didn't want to be a total liar.

"Who knows?" I thought. It might actually help.

I put on an old pair of green sweatpants and my green hoodie, laced up my Asics Gels and headed outside. By the time I reached the street, the rain had turned to a light mist. I watched as the car headlights gently caressed the wet, black asphalt making it shiny. Just like the Baretta.

I glanced across the street to see a young guy. Well, I thought he was young because I couldn't see any gray in his hair. It was hard to tell though. His body was all twisted and contorted, his head held immobile by a brace as he blew into the straw that made his wheelchair move. I watched as he got to the corner to wait for the light and I saw him…smile. What in the hell did he have to smile about? He was going to be confined to that chair, to that life, until he took his last breath.

I thought about how close I had come to his predicament. The car accident. The numbness in my hands feet and chest. The emergency room doctor telling me that vertebrae in my neck was pressed against my spinal cord and they'd have to go in through my throat to fix it or I'd be a quadriplegic. The warning that there may have been permanent damage and my running days might be over. The spasms. The neck brace. The three months on the couch popping Vicodin and spinning my wheels. How close I'd come. How close.

What did he have to smile about? Maybe it was because he was paralyzed and couldn't feel anything. I hurt all over and was willing to anything to make the pain stop. He was lucky. He was numb.

I trotted up the street at a good clip. There was an occasional tingling in my extremities. A lingering effect of the surgery. I was running though. The damage hadn't had long lasting effects. As I broke into a sprint, my mind began to wonder. I knew how I wanted to end it, but there were still questions that I needed to answer.

Once the ten days were up and I got the Beretta, where would I do it? Home? No. The kids would find me. Out in the wooded area behind our house? No good. It could be months before I was found. I had no desire to be a Discovery Channel documentary. I played with the idea of doing something original, like standing on the railing of the Golden Gate Bridge and shooting myself so that I fell into the water. I'd be a jumper and a shooter at the same time. The ultimate multitasker. I *did* know that the bullet would pierce my heart. That was the place that hurt the most.

I finished my three mile run and made my way home, my body a cocktail of sweat and raindrops. I walked into the front room where Carolyn sat on the couch reading a script for the spring musical at school. How she loved the theater.

"Hi Daddy," she said.

"Hi Sweetie. How was school?"

"Okay. What's for dinner?"

I thought for a moment.

"Chinese," I said. "I thought I would order some Chinese."

INTERLUDE: LEO'S STORY

As told to the author

I first tried to kill myself about forty years ago, when I was 18. Over a girl. It took me about ten seconds to chicken out and tell my father. I said, "Dad, we gotta go to the hospital. I just took a handful of pills and I don't want to die. I *did* want to die, but I don't now."

The old man says, "Okay. I'll give you a ride. But first you're going down to that school to confront that girl *and* her new boyfriend."

How crazy is that? I'm looped out of my head on drugs. I go down to the school, I tell the girl what I did and she looks at me like she just stepped in dog shit or something.

The boyfriend says, "We'd better get you to the hospital."

So, they take me to the hospital where they give me ipecac, which makes me throw up everything I'd eaten since the fourth grade.

The doctor says, "Keep him awake for the next twelve hours."

So the boyfriend stays with me all night long, walking me

up and down the hallways, around the hospital room. Finally I say, "Why you doin' this?" The son of a bitch slapped me across the face. Hard.

"Sorry," he says. "You were dozing off. And…you deserved it."

He was right. I did deserve it.

"Why you doin' this?" I say again. The bastard slapped me again.

"Because my mother died the same way," he says. "Now shut up and walk."

Who knew?

After a while, the girl was gone, but him…he was my best friend til the day he died. About three years ago. Stroke.

My parents divorced when I was five. Not a nice divorce either. You know what the court did? They took me, my brother and my sister, and put us in the middle of a room. Then, they put Mom on one side, Dad on the other side and said, "Choose who you wanna live with."

I was at that age where I was kinda clingy, ya know? So I ran and grabbed my mother's leg. My sister grabbed the other leg. My brother says, "But now Dad's gonna be all alone". He went with him. And *that's* how they split up the family. "Kids are re-silient". You've heard that right? Well it's a bunch of self-serving bullshit. Just adults rationalizing the shitty things their doing.

I'm sorry Brian. It's hard talking about this stuff, ya know? Alright, I didn't have the best childhood. Childhood was tough, but I "overcame" like you people say. By the way, I didn't mean nothing by that.

Things eventually got better. I got married, house, kids. Good job. New York Fire Department. Me and my brother.

Things were going pretty good. Then, the wife starts nagging me to move out here to California because it's warmer.

"Aren't you tired of scraping ice off the windshield every winter?" she says.

I *was* tired of scraping ice off the windshield. So, we move out here, I get a job with the department and again, things are going pretty good.

Then, this one night, I have this dream. I'm in the World Trade Center, north tower, in an elevator when the plane hits. The whole building comes down around me, and I'm dead. *I'm dead.* I never died in a dream before. I'm dead. It was so real. The smells, the sounds, the textures. I woke up screaming. I know that sounds like a cliché, but it's true. Scared the shit out of my wife. Now, here's the thing. This was in 2007. Six years after 9/11. And on that morning, I wasn't within three thousand miles of the World Trade Center. But my brother was.

Why am I dreaming about a disaster I wasn't even in? Well, the wife says I changed after that. I didn't get along with nobody. Nobody. My poor kid accidentally brought home decaf coffee from the store instead of regular, I tore her head off. I lost interest in everything, and I do mean everything. Even sex. That's when the wife knew something was up because...I wasn't. I can't find no pleasure in my work my kids. Nothing. So I start thinking, "Maybe this is as far as I'm supposed to go. Maybe this is it for me." Now, did I actually make plans to check out? Let's just say that I considered and rejected a number of different things. The wife finally gets me to go to the doctor, he puts me on some medicine and, it's working. I'm feeling pretty good.

About eight months go by, I convince myself I'm cured and stop taking the medicine. God damned delusional. Right up to the morning I curled up on the bathroom floor crying. "Go confront the girl. Go confront the guy." I'm a grown ass man and I ain't confronting nothing. Amanda, my wife God love her, sits down on the floor next to me. She holds my head in her lap saying, "It's okay, baby. It's alright."

Well, I'm back on the medicine. Gonna be taking it the rest of my life, I've resigned myself to *that* fact. Am I cured? Let's just say it's "under control".

CHAPTER 4

Day 3

A fter another restless night, I had somehow fallen asleep on the couch in my street clothes. Even though it seemed as though I possessed no trait other than lethargy, slumber came in fits and starts and, it was never enough to make me feel rested. I glanced at the cable remote on the coffee table in front of me. Maybe I could lose myself in the mindlessness of daytime television for a while. I picked it up, aimed it at the Comcast cable box and pressed ON. It was as though the stations were programming specifically for me.

Click: Dr. Phil sat lecturing a middle aged woman who sat sobbing into a handkerchief. "You can't keep somebody's suicidal feelings a secret," he said.

Click: A commercial. "Prozac may not be for everyone. Side effects may include drowsiness, upset stomach, erectile..."

Click: Oprah talking to a pop music star. "So you were in that abyss? That darkness?"

Jesus.

I pressed the power button and the television went black just as my cellphone lit up.

"Hello," I said.

"Hi Mr. Copeland," a highly charged, energetic Romper Room voice said on the other end. "It's Marci calling from the high school."

"Oh, hi Marci," I said warmly. I had no idea who this woman was.

"We're all so excited that you're going to come down and speak to us today," she said.

I am??

"Yeah," I said confused. "Me too."

"The kids have all read your book and they have so many questions," she enthused. "We can't wait to hear your motivational speech."

Silence on my end.

"Mr. Copeland?"

"Uh, yeah. Motivational speech. I can't wait to give it," I stammered.

"We have a space reserved for you in the teachers' lot. See you about 11:30. I'm the luckiest student activities coordinator in the entire world!" She gushed.

"Yes," I said. "I'll see you then."

I pressed the button ending the call. Motivational speech? Me? The way I was feeling at that moment? I checked my calendar and sure as shit, I had agreed to talk to three hundred high school kids at twelve o'clock. I used all the strength I could muster, got off the couch, showered, shaved and got dressed. I hopped in the car and headed for the school.

The high school that had invited to speak was in one of the

tony neighborhoods in the Bay Area. It was one of those schools that, although public, based upon the accoutrements available to the school community, the uninitiated would mistake it for private. A public school whose taxpayer based budget was supplemented by funds raised and donated by the wealthy residents of the area. The best public education money could buy.

My mind flashed back ten years to my days as co-host of the local FOX affiliate's morning show. I had been asked by one of my colleagues to emcee an auction at her son's public school in the Silicon Valley. Parents were raising funds to buy new equipment for the junior high computer lab. I agreed to do it as I am always happy to do what I can for the cause of education. I had filled the role of emcee at my kids' annual catholic school auction for years. On a good year, the donations of A's and Giants tickets baseball tickets, dinners at local restaurants and class projects might raise thirty or thirty-five thousand dollars.

At this auction, the items included a donation from rock legend Neil Young of lunch and a recording session with him in his home studio, a weekend at the private island of a software billionaire including round trip transportation in his private jet and a European holiday for six pledged by a local entrepreneur. By the time the auction ended, over two million dollars had been raised. *TWO MILLION DOLLARS* to supplement the budget of a *public* school. I couldn't help but think of the story our television station had run that morning of the public elementary school in a poor Oakland neighborhood whose boys' bathroom had been closed for two years because the school didn't have funds for the necessary repairs.

As I approached the school, I saw signs designating two parking lots. STUDENTS and TEACHERS. The students' lot looked like the showroom of a luxury car dealership with its Porches, Mercedes and BMWs. One fortunate little tyke even drove a bright yellow Ferrari. Who the hell gives a high school kid a Ferrari as a daily driver?

If the students' lot was a car show, the teachers' parking area was more like a used car place. Prius, Honda, Hyundai and the occasional Ford dotted the landscape. Whereas the kids were driving late model vehicles, their working class instructors had cars that averaged in the five-year range. This disparity bothered me.

Teaching is, in my opinion, the most important profession in our society. Without teachers there are no doctors, no lawyers, no scientists, artists or engineers. That being the case, why do we value them and their contributions so little? If I were king of the world, teaching would be our highest paid profession. I'd certainly compensate them better than professional athletes, hedge fund managers and reality TV stars.

One parking place was blocked off with a construction barricade with a bouquet of helium balloons tethered to it, dancing in the wind. Next to the space stood a young girl. She looked to be about 15. She had her hair in a ponytail, adorned with a ribbon that matched the school colors on the Letterman's jacket she wore. The bright colors in her attire were nothing compared to the grin on her face. It was a big, bright, exuberant smile. The kind that pisses you off when you see it and you aren't in a good mood.

The girl waved her arms frantically as she jumped up and down, her ponytail bouncing with excitement. I slid into the parking space, turned off the motor and was barely out of the car when she descended upon me.

"Hi Mr. Copeland. I'm Robin! I'm your student representative!" She gushed.

Jesus. Did *everybody* at this school take their peppy pills this morning?

"It's an honor to meet you sir!" She enthused.

"Likewise," I said. "And don't call me 'sir'. I'm not Sidney Poitier."

"Who?" She said.

Seriously? *Seriously*??

"*To Sir With Love*," I said in an attempt to help her out. "*Guess Who's Coming To Dinner?*"

"I give up," she said. "Who's coming to dinner."

I resisted the urge to make an Abbott and Costello reference because I knew that she had no idea who they were either.

"Lead on," I said.

Robin led me through the parking lot into the office where a sixty something woman behind the counter directed me to sign in with my name and my time of arrival. After I'd done so, I was handed a yellow adhesive name tag with my name on it and the word VISITOR in bold black letters. I was instructed to put the tag on the vest pocket of my sport coat. I nodded and then followed Robin out of the office while slipping the name tag into my pants pocket. I was not putting adhesive on an Armani sport coat for anybody.

The girl led me through the locker lined hallway. Even her walk was chipper.

"So," I said, "What'd you letter in?"

"I'm the captain of the woman's soccer team," she chirped. "We're five and one this season!"

"Cool. That's very cool," I said, nodding.

She was like Kelly Ripa on steroids.

We soon reached a dark, wood grained door with the words TEACHER LOUNGE. Robin knocked and I walked in where I was almost tackled.

"Oh Mr. Copeland! We're so happy you can be here with us today!"

Marci was a compact little dynamo. She was about 5'5" tall with short dark hair and an energy that could have only come from drinking coffee laced with meth and five-hour energy drinks.

"The kids are all assembled in the auditorium. We're so happy you can be here with us today."

Robin led me out of the teachers' lounge, down the hallway and across the quad area to the auditorium. We entered through a side stage door and stood in the wings. A young male teacher stood onstage addressing the students about decorum, cell phones, texting, etcetera. I didn't really hear anything coming out of his mouth because I was fixated on his tan corduroy sport coat with patches on the elbows. Now, I'm not exactly a GQ magazine cover model but…corduroy?? Really?? Hey dude, the seventies called. They want their clothes back.

"All right, settle down," he said to the chattering kids. "You all know are speaker so I'm just gonna bring him out now. Please welcome, Mr. Brian Copeland."

I came out to polite applause. The kids had apparently been assigned my book, *Not a Genuine Black Man*, which deals with racial identity and my childhood growing up in San Leandro, California in the 1970s when it was over 90% white and considered by Fair Housing advocates to be a "racist bastion of white supremacy". Millennials are shocked that racism and prejudice could have been so overt and so blatant in the Bay Area. To them, the 1970s is as ancient as the 1920s were to me at that age.

I talked to kids a bit. Told them how I came to write *Genuine* as a book and a solo play. I told them stories that hadn't been included in the book. Then I took their questions.

"Did you hate the kids that picked on you when you were younger?"

"No," I said. "You hate them, they win."

"How do I become a big success in life like you?"

Like me.

"Your success in life will always be in direct proportion to what you do *after* you do what's expected of you."

"On Gilligan's Island, who was hotter? Ginger or Mary Ann?"

"Ginger. Guys only say Mary Ann so that they don't look shallow."

"Is it true that you were once so depressed that you wanted to kill yourself?"

I wrote in the book about what was later described as a suicide 'gesture' I had made in a fit of despair in 1999. The question wasn't as surprising as the kid who asked it. Robin. Little Miss Rah Rah. Robin, whose biggest concern in life was what color to pick for her prom dress.

"Yes," I said. "It's true."

I paused and took in the silence. Three hundred kids, not moving, chatting, whispering or texting. Three hundred kids suddenly looking at me with rapt attention.

"I have this...disease," I said. "It's called Depression. It's a nasty, nasty disease because, it's like there's this voice whispering in your ear...and it's trying to kill you."

I could see a girl in the front row wipe her eyes and then stare at her lap.

"From what I read, statistically, there are a lot of 'us' here. A lot of you hear that little voice. If you do, it's very important that you tell somebody. A teacher, parent, counselor, friend... somebody. Because if you don't, believe me...it *will* kill you."

I finished my talk, thank my hosts and followed Robin back out to my car.

"I really enjoyed your talk," she said.

She looked at me and smiled. For the first time since I met her, I looked at her. I mean *really* looked at her. Her smile was forced. Despite her peppy, bubbly demeanor, her eyes looked... sad.

"You're one of 'us' aren't you."

The fake smile faded. She nodded her head.

"Do you think about hurting yourself, Sweetie?"

She looked at the ground, then back at me. No more covering.

"Sometimes," she said.

"Have you told anybody? Does anybody know?"

Her eyes shifted back to the asphalt beneath her feet.

"No," she whispered.

She suddenly reminded me of myself when I was her age. I was in plays, always running for office. I was the king of school spirit. I was jovial, and a joker. The life of the party. Inside, I was lonely, sad, isolated. I was filled with self-loathing and suicidal more days than not. It's a miracle I made it through those years. Nobody ever *really* looked at me like I was now looking at this girl.

"Can I tell somebody?" I said softly.

She had shifted her gaze from the ground to the sky. It was as though she was trying to pull some answer from the clouds.

"Please?" I said.

"Okay," she whispered.

We headed back into the building, down the hall and back to the Teachers' Lounge. I entered and left the door open so that I could keep an eye on Robin who hovered in front of it. I was afraid she might take off. I know that's what I'd have done.

"Oh Mr. Copeland," Marci said, still gushing. I wondered what *her* exuberance was hiding. "Can't stay away from us can you?"

"Marci," I began shifting my glance between her and the troubled kid in front of the door. "You have a problem. Robin is...ill."

"Oh, that darned bug has been going around school for the last three weeks now," She said, shaking her head.

"No, you don't understand. She's ill...in my way," I said. "Look, I think that she's a very depressed kid and she needs somebody to talk to her."

Marci glanced at Robin.

"Well, I certainly appreciate your concern, but I know my kids a lot better than you do," she said, dismissively. "Robin has a 4.3 grade point average, she's the captain of the women's soccer team and..."

"And she's gonna be dead one of these days if you don't do something," I said, cutting her off.

What is with this notion that because a person is accomplished or successful in some outward manner that they must be well adjusted and happy inwardly? Some of the happiest people I've ever met were also some of the saddest.

"I'm sorry," I said. "That was harsh."

Marci sighed, looked at me and then at the door.

"Robin, would you come in here for a moment please?" She said.

Robin stepped inside the room and shut the door behind her. All traces of her former effervescence were gone.

"Would you like to have some lunch with me today?" Marci said.

"Sure," came the barely audible reply.

My job was done.

"You take care kiddo," I said to the girl. "And remember, your soccer team wouldn't be five and one...without you."

She gave me a faint smile before I turned around, walked out to the parking lot, got into my car and drove away, shaking my head at the hypocrite I was. What would that poor kid think when she found out that I didn't take my own advice? Be that as it may, I had saved her life. I got her to tell somebody, to open up and talk about the demon raging inside. That should be enough. Then again, I know about another teenage boy who told his parents. They listened. They tried to understand. They did everything they could to help. Right up to the day they found his hanging from the light fixture in his bedroom.

I told that story during a talk I was giving one night and was cornered after the speech by an African American man a few years older than me.

"You was talkin' bout a white kid, right? It was a white kid did that,' he asked.

"What difference does it make?" I said.

"Cuz black people don't do shit like that. White people is fucked up," he said, shaking his head.

"Sure, we all know that there's no mental illness in the black community," I said, my sarcasm apparent.

He wasn't letting this bone go.

"Who dies more by suicide?" He ranted. "Who kills themselves more? Black people or white people? I'll tell you who... white people."

Alright, I have to admit that he had a point there.

"Ok," I said, "Let's flip it around. Who dies more from *homicide?* Black people or white people? Black people."

This irritated him.

"Quit changing the subject", he shouted. "White people is fucked up."

"No. They're depressed."

"Depressed?" He said, incredulity dripping from the word. "Why? They own every motherfuckin' thing in the world. Shit. They fucked up. Abraham Lincoln was fucked up."

"Abraham Lincoln suffered from depression," I corrected.

"He was fucked up!" The man shouted. "That's the only reason we free! The next time you look at a five-dollar bill, just think, Abraham Lincoln...fucked up."

I shook my head. He wasn't done.

"You fond of gravity? Isaac Newton...fucked up! The Nutcracker? Tchaikovsky...fucked up!"

He was on a roll.

"Mark Twain...fucked up! Teddy Roosevelt...fucked up! Winston Churchill...fucked up! Richard Nixon...*really* fucked up!"

How do I get myself trapped in these situations?

"Mother Teresa..." he continued. "Alright, not her...but I had you goin' there for a minute didn't I?"

CHAPTER 5

Day 4

It was dusk. I had watched the cool darkness give way to the breaking dawn, then turn to the heat of the noonday sun. Now, I watched as the sun morphed into the amber color of molten lava as it prepared to make way for the moon's shift. I had been in bed all day. Getting up would have required both strength and desire. At that moment, I had neither. I was just lying there. Watching reruns of *Three's Company*. It was the episode where the roommates all had this *big* misunderstanding.

The cellphone on my nightstand glowed. Blocked number.

"Hello," I said.

"Duuuude," said the voice on the other end. Why was this guy working in a gun shop? No openings at the medical marijuana dispensary?

"Dude," he said. "I've got good news dude. Your background check came back all clean. What do you have to say about that?'

"Allahu Akbar," I said.

"What?"

"Nothing," I replied. I was glad he didn't get it. It was in bad taste. "So what happens now?"

"Well," he said, "You can come down and pick up the weapon as soon as the waiting period is up in..."

I could hear him shuffling papers, consulting a calendar.

"Six days," he said. "On that day, what time do you want to come in and pick up the weapon?"

"Oh," I said. I hadn't really thought about it. "Um..."

"Dude, something wrong?"

"Sorry, I'm distracted," I said. "I'm watching *Three's Company*."

"Duuude! I *love* that show!!!," he beamed. "Did you ever see the one where they all had this big misunderstanding?"

"No, I think I missed that one."

"Well, what time do you want to pick up the weapon? That day I should be here from nine 'til six. I might leave in the afternoon for a minute to get a burrito..."

"Nine," I said. "I'll be there at nine."

"Okay," He paused for minute. "Dude, you gotta tell me what channel *Three's Company* is on. I *love* that show!"

I told him. As I clicked the phone off, there was a knock at my bedroom door.

"Daddy, it's Carolyn," she said softly. "Can I come in?"

I wanted to be alone. It was all about isolating.

"Yeah," I said. "Come on in."

The door opened and Carolyn walked in. She looked tired. Dark crescent moons were beginning to form under her eyes.

"Daddy, you're still in bed. It's dinner time."

"I know," I said without looking at her. "I ordered some Chinese."

"Do you want some when it gets here?"

"No, you guys go on ahead," I said. "Just put the leftovers in the refrigerator."

She paused. I could tell that she was searching for words.

"Daddy...," she said. "I went to the cemetery today. I saw your mom. And Grandma."

I nodded.

—

She seemed so much younger than her sixteen years at that moment. I thought back to the days I co-hosted the local FOX morning television program. I'd get home around 11 in the morning most days. Carolyn was around four and as soon as I'd walk in the door, she'd come running to me.

"Daddeeeee!" She'd squeal as she leaped into my arms. I'd pick her up and squeeze her tight. She'd kiss me on the cheek.

"I missed you Daddy!" She'd say. I wondered if she missed me now.

" Your mom and Grandma...they're very worried about you," she said.

"Yeah," I said, staring at my lap.

"Grandma wants me to give you a message," she said.

I looked at my hands as if there was some wisdom to be found in them.

"Daddy, look at me," she said.

My jerked up and I looked her in the eye.

"What?" I said clinched teeth.

"Grandma said to tell you, '*Get your ass up. Get your black ass up now'!*"

At a previous low point in my life, Grandma had motivated me to get up and keep going with those words. I portray the incident in *Not a Genuine Black Man*. Carolyn traveled with me while I was on tour and saw the show over four hundred times.

"Daddy, did you hear me?" She said.

I looked back down at my hands.

"I'm sorry Sweetie, but that's not going to work this time," I said. "Not this time."

She exhaled. Frustrated. Exasperated.

"Alright then, you listen to me," she said, the little girl gone. "All my life, you've been ten feet tall to me. You've been my hero. Don't let this beat you Daddy. Don't."

"I'm sorry I let you down kid," I said.

"You only let me down if you don't try. You've never let me down before, don't do it now," She said. Tears were forming in her eyes.

"Try daddy," she said. "Try."

As I watched her walk out the door, it was only then, for the first time, that I truly realized how hard all of this was on her. How hard it had been on all three of them. It was definitely not my finest moment.

Did you ever wish that you could jump into a time machine, go back and slap the shit out of yourself? I sometimes think about what I might say to my depressed self if I could step outside of my body and confront him?

"Grow up. It's time to put your big boy pants on," wouldn't work. I could try asking him, "Don't you know how lucky you are? You're young. You're healthy. You've got a full head of hair and most of your teeth." That would almost certainly have no effect. I could rattle off the list of "could be's", telling him, "You could be hungry. You could be homeless. You could be crippled. You could be in Syria." I know that he would sit there.

I could then try anger. I could yell at him, *"What is wrong with you?* Don't you see what you're doing to that poor kid? She's sixteen years old and she has to baby her dad? And what do you think will happen to these kids when you're gone? I'll tell you what. They will spend the rest of their lives blaming themselves for not saving YOU. Do you really want to saddle them with that? You say that you love them. That's not love, that's sick. You're sick! *You're sick!"*

I could try that, but it wouldn't work. He wouldn't be able to hear me because...he's sick.

CHAPTER 6

People who are not super religious generally go to church on three occasions; Christmas, Easter...and when they're really in trouble. I thought of this as I trudged up the steps of the church rectory. The prodigal son returns. I've always hated that story. The brother who goes off and blows half his father's fortune on booze and hookers gets a party just for coming back, while the brother who stayed home the whole time gets squat. That is a bullshit story.

I reached the front door and had balled my hand into a knocking fist when it opened and Father appeared. Father is a rotund man in his late sixties. He had on his coat and a touring cap. Funny, even without his collar exposed, he looked like a priest. I like him. He's a good guy and a spiritual man. A true priest in this age of those who desecrate the collars they wear and make a mockery of the vows they've taken. Father literally restored my faith in the institution of the priesthood and, by extension, the Catholic Church itself.

"Oh, Brian," he said. I had startled him. "How are you?"

"I'm sorry Father. I see you're going out. I'll come back another time."

I turned to leave.

He stopped me with a hand on my shoulder.

"No," he said. *"How ARE you?"*

I turned and looked at him. He has a kind face. He was truly asking the question. And not in a perfunctory way.

"Not so good," I said.

"Come in. We'll talk," he said, his hand now on my back guiding me inside.

We walked down the short hallway of the rectory into the livingroom area. It was a soothing room. The walls were paneled with the warm tones of rich, brown wood. Two mahogany tables with plain white lamps sat at both sides of a floral designed couch. It reminded me of the furniture I'd see at my great grandfather's home when I was a little boy. All that was missing was the old people's smell.

Father sat in one of two brown leather chairs facing the flowered couch. He motioned for me to sit and I did, moving a rose adorned pillow to the side.

"So," he said, "What's on your mind?"

I looked at my lap.

"The story of the prodigal son," I said.

"What about it?"

"Well," I said, "The brother who stayed home got screwed."

"What do you mean?"

"He stayed home and he took care of business. He did what he was supposed to do. What was expected of him. He didn't do anything wrong or disrespectful to his father like his brother did. Where's his fatted calf?"

Father ran his fingers through thinning hair.

"It's a story about forgiveness," he said.

"Well, the brother who stayed home sure as hell didn't need any forgiveness," I said, anger creeping into my voice.

"We *all* need forgiveness," he said.

I began to pick at a hangnail on my right ring finger.

"Is that all?" He asked.

Silence.

"Brian?" He prodded.

"I'm...I'm thinking about maybe..." I looked up from my lap and into his eyes. "Doing myself in."

It was the first time I'd actually said out loud what I'd been thinking all this time. It was almost a little liberating to articulate the plan. To share with another person the torture I'd been hiding in keeping my own counsel.

He gently nodded and said, "I see."

I don't know how I expected him to react. I do know that the expectation wasn't the calm, unexcited response he gave me.

"Well," I said, "Give me some Catholic mumbo jumbo about why I shouldn't do that."

He smiled.

"Now you know I don't operate that way," he said.

"Well, tell me what the bible says."

I immediately realized that this was a dumb thing to say. We're Catholic. We don't read the bible. We read the missatlette. That's like the Cliff's Notes to the bible.

He thoughtfully stroked his chin.

"Why do you want to take your life?"

My eyes began to water.

"Because I hurt all over," I said. I began to sob. "I hurt all over and no matter what I do it won't stop and I can't do this anymore. I can't. I can't *I can't.*"

I had completely broken down. Father nodded. We sat in silence for a moment.

"Then why tell me," he finally said.

"I don't know," I said, frustrated. "I don't know."

He couldn't help me. This was a mistake. I got up angrily and headed for the door. I was reaching for the doorknob to leave when Father got up and crossed over to me. I didn't know that he could move that fast.

"Wait, wait, wait," he said.

I stopped and looked at him. His eyes were contemplative.

"Tell me," he said. "Have you ever walked the labyrinth at the convent?"

"Labyrinth?" I said.

"Yes. It's a quest in the form of a maze. You walk the labyrinth and ponder a question. By the time you reach the center, you will find illumination."

Great, I'm suicidal and he's giving me Dungeons and Dragons shit.

"Walk the labyrinth and think. *Really think* about why you want to do this."

"Labyrinth," I scoffed as I turned and again grabbed for the door handle."

I felt his hand on my shoulder. I stopped.

"And Brian," he said.

I turned to face him.

"As dark a place as the world might seem right now," he said. "It would be a lot darker without *you* in it."

There was something about the way he said it. Like what happened to me mattered. Like *I* mattered.

"*Try Daddy. Try.*"

I nodded.

"Labyrinth," I whispered.

I opened the door and left.

CHAPTER 7

Day 6

Mercy Center is a conference and retreat complex located in the city of Burlingame, about fifteen miles south of San Francisco. The forty-acre facility is sponsored by the Sisters of Mercy and includes a convent, chapel, dining and sleeping quarters and a Catholic girls' school on its grounds. I had stayed there once on a private retreat once in the late 90s. It was a good place to walk, pray and think. A place to find center. Close, yet still far enough away from the outside world to get perspective. As I drove through the ornate front gate and into the parking lot, I thought about how much peace I had found on my last visit during another troubled time in my life.

I parked and walked into the main building. A grand-motherly woman sat behind the information counter sorting brochures. I love Catholic volunteers. They're generally retired folks trying to stay busy and give back to society at the same time. As I approached, the woman smiled.

"Good morning," she said.

She was cheerful. Sometimes, cheerful the last thing on earth you want to hear when you're depressed.

"Can you please tell me where I can find the labyrinth?" I asked.

She smiled again. It seemed as though everybody else in the world had a reason to smile.

"You just cross the parking lot and follow the path to the garden," she said. "You can't miss it."

I thanked her and turned toward the door.

"Here," she said, handing me a pamphlet. "This will explain how it works spiritually."

Spirituality is another thing you want no part of when you're deep in the hole. I've never considered myself to be a religious person. Not really. Others may disagree because I *do* believe in God and I pray. When the demon has me, I feel all alone. As though God has "forsaken me" as his boy once said. Although people who suffer from depression have told me that they find some comfort and solace in prayer and meditation, up to this point in time, it hadn't worked well for me. I think it's in large part because when I'm deeply depressed, I can't focus. My mind wanders and my thoughts are scattered. When I *am* able to think about one thing, it's generally some problem or potential problem that I'm fixated on in an unhealthy way. And then, I catastrophize it, playing out the "worse case scenario" over and over. This, of course, deepens my depression making matters in my head worse. It truly is a vicious cycle.

I made my way along the path, past neatly trimmed shrubs and brightly colored flowers. One for every Crayola in the 64 box. Soon, I came to the clearing where the labyrinth was. It was a maze alright. A dirt path that zigged and zagged. It reminded me of the puzzles in the books Grandma used to buy us at the grocery store to keep us occupied during long car trips. It was in a circular design with what appeared to be small pieces or wood, maybe two or three inches high, delineating each route. The piece of cheese in the middle of this thing was a great big jagged aquamarine colored rock.

I opened the pamphlet and read:

"The labyrinth has been a form of meditation for over 3500 years and is believed to contain mystical powers."

"Great," I thought. Again with the *Star Wars*.

I read on.

"There are no tricks and there are no dead ends. All paths eventually lead to the center, and that's where the answers are."

I stood looking across the pathway at the rock. This was ridiculous. New Age bullshit. I turned to walk back to the car, and the I stopped myself. I was here after all. I'd gotten in the car and driven the 45 miles from home to walk this thing. I had nothing to lose and nothing better to do.

"What the hell," I said to myself. "I'll walk towards the blue rock."

I stuffed the pamphlet and my car keys in my pockets and walked to the mouth of the maze. The noon day sun shined bright above me as I stepped onto the path. I felt silly. At least there was no one else walking. I had it all to myself.

I stared at my shadow on the ground as I began to wind my way through the puzzle. Father had said that I should ponder a question. I thought for a minute and then whispered, "Why do I hurt so much?"

"Why do I hurt so much," I said over and over.

The answer came in a flurry. I hurt because I totaled my

sports car. I loved that car. The path took me to the left, cut off and shifted to the right. The rock was behind me now. A big blue obelisk taunting me in the corner of my eye. Blue. Like me for weeks now. Months now. Unable to make sense out of anything. I followed as it took another left moving the stone to my right. I hurt because my wife took off and never even gave me a reason. I hurt because it triggered all of the abandonment I had felt all my life. My mother dying when I was fourteen. A father who was abusive when he was around which, thank God, wasn't often. Now, Grandma left me too. Grandma who was never supposed to die. Grandma who was too tough, too strong and resilient to pass away did just that. How do I live in a world where even that pillar is not a constant? I felt the sting of angry tears burn my eyes. This is stupid. I don't want to do this. I'm not doing this anymore. I'm going to get the hell out of here.

Carolyn's words reverberated in my head.

Try Daddy. Try.

"Try, Daddy," I whispered.

I drew in a deep breath and wiped tears from my eyes.

"Why do I feel that my life is worthless?" I whispered.

I began to walk again. This time, the road bent rightward.

"Why do I feel my that life is worthless?"

A white puffy cloud moved across the sky, obscuring the sun. My shadow on the ground faded as I turned right, then left, then a longer path to the right.

"Why do I feel that my life is worthless?"

A short right brought me to the base of the rock, where I collapsed in a fit of tears.

"Because it's my fault. It's all my fault. Every horrible thing that's happened is because of me. All of it. *I'm being punished because it's all my fault."*

And there it was. Finally. The truth. I had confronted my-self. There was something inherently bad about me. I was a bad person and it was for that reason that I had been suffering. It was for that reason that I had to die. As I said before, this was a mind that was not giving me accurate information. A demon whispering in my ear that was trying to kill me. Taking it all apart and, as Father had said, *really thinking* about why I wanted to harm myself opened things up for me. I received clarity. A bright, shining light through all of the haze and white noise that had been whirling about my head for what seemed like forever. I realized what was really happening. In that moment, I finally got it.

It wasn't my fault. None of it. Accidents happen. They just do. People leave sometimes and there is nothing you can do about it. They just go. As for Grandma…I had to face the reality that it was just her time. As monumental a figure as she was in my life, as essential as she was to my very existence, she was only human, and as such, we all face our time to leave this Earth. Like it or not. Ready or not. It was Grandma's time.

It wasn't my fault. There was no Divine Retribution here. I was believing the lies that the disease was feeding me. Listening to the false information and taking it to heart. Father had said that everyone needs forgiveness. It was time for me to forgive myself. It wasn't my fault. I wasn't to blame for the Job like series of misfortunes that had befallen me. Most importantly, it wasn't my fault that I was sick.

"It's isn't my fault," I whispered, the stream of tears slowing. "It isn't my fault."

No. It isn't.

INTERLUDE: CHARLIE REDUX

As told to the author

They said I had seventy-seven cuts on my arm. Seventy-seven. Funny, it didn't seem like many. I had to talk to doctors and counselors and they're all, "Why are you so sad?" I'm all, "I'm not sad." They're all, "Yes you are." I'm all, "No I'm not." They're all, "Why do you cut yourself then?" I didn't really have a good answer for that one. Why couldn't I have been bulimic instead? Then at least I could fit in those skinny jeans at the mall.

I had to stay out of school for a whole month. They let me work from home. Told all the kids I had mono. My friend Jill told people I got it from Richard just to piss Shelly off. Dr. Jerry, he's my therapist. He says I cut myself to focus my pain. Funny, I didn't know I had any pain. But I guess I do. Because of Mom. The good news is, I haven't cut myself in a whole year. My arm's all healed. Sure, I feel like it sometimes. DJ, that's my nickname for Dr. Jerry. DJ says that when I want to cut, it's my anxiety. Now, when I feel anxiety, I do other stuff. I go to the gym. Dad turned the extra bedroom into an art studio and I go work on my paintings. I still have to have therapy with DJ twice a week, but that's okay. He's cool. I even did a painting for him. It's of a guy cutting a girl in half with a sword. The girl looks just like Shelly.

I know. Kinda dark huh?

CHAPTER 8

Days 7–9

The proof of one's sanity lies not in whether you take medication, or you see a doctor or therapist. It's in how you relate to people. How you relate to others, but most importantly, how you relate to yourself. Father told me that. Like I said, he gets it. You see, Father is one of us too.

I was not "cured" by my epiphany at the labyrinth, but I *was* "healed." Spiritually on some level. The meditative exercise of asking myself the hard questions while making the physical journey along the maze helped me to come to some understanding of what was going on with me. It allowed the voice of reason to speak loudly enough for me to hear it.

I left Mercy Center feeling better than I had in months. I went home and showered. This was something else that had been irregular during the depths of the sadness. I then cleaned my room and made the bed. It's strange how something as mundane as doing household chores can make you feel "normal." The following day, I went to the gym and for four miles

on the treadmill. I was able to move at a pace close to what I had
been able to run before the surgery. The effects of the accident
wouldn't be long lasting. But sleep was sporadic. When I was
able to sleep, it was a restful slumber. Not one tortured by night-
mares or induced by a thorough lack of physical and emotional
energy.

A few days after the labyrinth, I had a dream that had a
profound effect on me.

> *I stood in front of a park bench. My mother looked up at me*
> *and smiled. Grandma sat to her right and she was smiling*
> *too. Tears streamed down my cheeks and I bent over, hugged*
> *Grandma and squeezed her with all my might.*
> *"I miss you so much," I said. "So much."*
> *She squeezed me back. Then, after what felt like both a brief*
> *moment and an eternity…she let me go.*
> *"Now," she said placing a gentle hand on my shoulder, "Go*
> *on."*
> *My mother said nothing. She grinned.*
> *"Go on," Grandma said. "Go on. Go on."*
> *The light got brighter and brighter and I opened my eyes.*

They were wet, the result of weeping in my sleep. I lay there
as the sun peeked through the Venetian blinds in my room.
Bathing my face. Making it warm.

"Go on," I heard ringing in my ears. "Go on. Go on.".

I had someplace to go.

Day 10

The Beretta in my hand felt heavier than it had before. I moved
it from my right hand to my left and examined the gun. The

object that I had been fixated on, obsessed with, didn't hold the same allure. I was holding a Christmas toy in January. The novelty had worn off. The surfer-tractor dude reached below the glass cabinet and retrieved a medium sized box.

"Here's your clip, dude," he said. "You're all good to go."

I looked at the box, then to the Beretta in my hand, then at the box again.

"Dude," he said, "Is something wrong?"

The Nugget Man stood in his usual spot in the corner space where two perpendicular glass cabinets met. He stared at me intently. Sizing me up.

"I don't need this man," I said, handing Surfer Dude the gun.

He looked at me for a minute, confused. Then, frustration washed over his face.

"Have you been talking to another dealer?" He said in a tone that let me know that this was apparently an ongoing problem.. "Have you been talking to another dealer behind my back? Dude, how could you do that to me? We had a relationship."

Jesus, he was a spurned lover.

"No," I said. "There's no other dealer."

"What then?" He demanded. "My weapons ain't good enough for you?"

"Look," I said, cutting him off. "It's not you, it's me. It's a perfectly lovely gun. I just don't need it anymore."

The Nugget Man spoke up.

"What about the problems in your neighborhood? They over?"

"I'm not so worried about my stuff anymore," I said.

He was silent for a moment as he stared into my eyes. It was as if he had something to say but wasn't quite sure if should say it.

"You know," he finally said, "These things come in waves. You ain't seen the last of this."

I nodded.

"Of that, " I said, "I can be certain."

—

The sun shone brightly as I walked out of the gun store toward the parking lot. No trace of the dark clouds that had filled the skies with rain over the previous weeks. I stood there for a moment, taking it all in. There is a scene in the 2006 movie, *Superman Returns,* where, after being hobbled by a kryptonite trap set by Lex Luthor, the Man of Steel soars high into the sky and bathes himself in the warmth of the sun's rays in order to recharge himself. I thought of that scene as I stretched my arms out wide, taking in the heat and light. I was feeling so many things in that moment. Unburdened. Energized. Alive.

I made my way home, parked the car and walked into the front room where I was greeted by Carolyn.

"Hi Daddy," she said.

"Hi Sweetie."

"How are you," she asked, apprehensive.

"Fine," I said softly. "I'm just fine."

She was suspicious.

"Yeah?" she said. "What's for dinner?"

I thought for a moment and then let out a big grin.

"Spaghetti," I said. "I am going to make you some spaghetti."

ACKNOWLEDGMENTS

As you can probably imagine, this was a challenging story to tell in its original form as a stage production. Getting the right tone as well as the right blend of comedy, drama and information in just the right doses was a bit of a magic trick. Transferring those ingredients to the written page in a way that preserved those elements was at times trying and I couldn't have done it alone. To that end, I'd like to thank my mentor, director, collaborator, father confessor and friend David Ford for sharing his gift for taking a story and presenting it in a way that is compelling, thought provoking and entertaining. You've changed my life and the direction of my work pal. I am forever in your debt.

I'd also like to thank my editor Dorothy Smith for her guidance in making the translation from spoken word to written word work. Thanks for the extra set of eyes and ears Dorothy.

Thank you to my beautiful life partner Teresa Cavazos for her love and support on this project and for sitting through about a hundred performances of the play. When you're spilling your guts on stage to strangers, it's nice to know that there's at least one friendly face in the audience. I love you.

Thank you to my managers, John Ferriter and Jamie Gruttemeyer for being there every step of the way. Thanks for believing.

Last, but certainly not least, thanks to my children Adam, Carolyn and Casey for never giving up on the old man during the dark times. I love you guys more than you'll ever know.

ABOUT THE AUTHOR

Brian Copeland is an award-winning actor, comedian, author, playwright, television and radio talk show host. He is the writer/performer of *NOT A GENUINE BLACK MAN*, the longest running solo play in San Francisco theatrical history and the author of the bestselling memoir of the same name. His other works include the play and novella, *THE JEWELRY BOX* and the solo plays *THE WAITING PERIOD* and *THE SCION*. *THE BRIAN COPELAND SHOW* can be heard weekday afternoons on KGO radio in San Francisco.

Brian Copeland lives in the San Francisco Bay Area.

Made in the USA
San Bernardino, CA
20 March 2018